Content

Illustrations

Joseph Blight. Page 3, 10, 18, 21

© Paul Atlas-Saunders. Page 6, 12

© Alex Langstone. Page 8

Ethel K. Burgess. Page 14, 17

John Alfred Harris. Page 19

Front Cover

Ladock church by Alex Langstone

Available soon….

From Granite to Sea ~
The Folklore of Bodmin Moor and East Cornwall

The first ever comprehensive focus on the folklore of eastern Cornwall. Alex Langstone's ground-breaking study will guide the reader through a myriad of old tales, supernatural encounters, amazing folk traditions and curious customs from the high moors, rugged clifftops, secret coves and lush estuaries across the eastern reaches of the Duchy. This title will be published by Troy Books, and will be available soon.

Lien Gwerin

A Journal of Cornish Folklore

Number 1

Compiled and edited by

Alex Langstone

Spirit of Albion Books

in association with

Cornish Folklore

Lien Gwerin a Gernow

www.cornishfolklore.co.uk

This collection published in 2017 by

Spirit of Albion Books, Cornwall, UK

www.spiritofalbionbooks.co.uk

in association with

Cornish Folklore ~ Lien Gwerin a Gernow

www.cornishfolklore.co.uk

ISBN 978-0-9563554-5-4

ISSN 2515-2483

With grateful thanks to:

Paul Atlas-Saunders, Andy Norfolk, Cheryl Straffon
and Craig Weatherhill

Saints, Demons and Conjurors

The village of Ladock lies in the heart of the mid-Cornwall countryside a few miles to the north-east of the city of Truro. The settlement is named after Lodoca, a 6th Century Irish Abbess, who, like so many of her contemporaries, came to Cornwall to set up a religious community. She is thought to have founded her settlement close to the holy well, at Fentonladock. There is an old story associated with her and her neighbouring missionaries, Grace and Probus. One day they all decided that the boundary between their two villages should be formally marked. They would each rise at dawn, and walk towards their neighbour's settlement, and where they met would be the new boundary. Probus set off at dawn, but Ladoca decided to brush her very long hair before she departed. By the time she had finished, Probus had almost arrived at Lodoca's settlement, hence the current parish boundaries uneven size.

Ladock Glebe holy well. on the valley floor below the church, is where water has traditionally been collected for baptisms, and this beautiful holy well sits in an enchanting green dell amid oak, holly and beech trees, with the church tower clearly visible on the hill to the south.

The village is also home to the amazing tales of Parson Wood, Ghost layer extraordinaire. William Wood was rector at Ladock between 1704 and 1749, a time when many Cornish clergy were involved in lavish exorcisms of demons and ghosts. Rev. Wood was a skilled exorcist, astrologer and

occultist and he was kept busy keeping many undesirable entities at bay. He was respected by all his parishioners and was at the heart of village life, being actively involved in the continued survival of traditional Cornish wrestling and hurling. He was the official keeper of the silver hurling ball, and encouraged the game in the parish. When out, the Parson would carry a fancy ebony walking stick. It had a massive silver finial on which was engraved a pentacle, and just below this, on the dark shaft of the stick was a band of silver, engraved with planetary symbols and mystical figures. He is famous for laying many ghosts and devils, and he was usually a match for most demons, whom he would change into animals and dispatch with his whip. However, one of his most famous exorcisms proved to be more problematic. This particular demon took the shape of a terrifying bird like figure that took the church tower as his home. The demon was very large with coal-black plumage and fiery eyes. The feathered fiend, which looked like no known bird, would make a hideous racket, which would bellow down the tower, petrifying the bell-ringers. The Parson was having trouble laying the demon by his usual methods, as he kept hiding behind the pinnacles on the tower, and Wood eventually devised a plan of exorcism using newly baptised children to rid the village of this noisy menace. He gathered nine unbaptised children to the church. Once baptised, the children were presented around the base of the tower along with mothers, who each held their children aloft, whilst Parson Wood walked around them all, muttering and cutting the air in various figures with his walking stick. The fiend eventually took flight, after one last prolonged screech, and he darted straight up flapping his dark and demonic wings, from which fiery sparks and flames of blue were seen billowing, as the demon headed for St Enoder. The

Ladock church. The location of many supernatural and demonic manifestations encountered by Parson William Wood

parson was also famous for foiling an attempt by the Devil to beat local Cornish wrestling hero John 'Jackey' Trevail at a clandestine midnight wrestling match on Le Pens Plat Common, and it was rumoured that the devil in question may have been sent by the neighbouring St Enoder witches, who could often be seen flying on their ragwort stems during the time of the full moon or heading home after their midnight meetings in the shape of hares.

There is mention of a "celebrated Ladock conjuror", in Richard Polwhele's *Traditions and Recollections volume 2, 1826.* This particular conjuror is reported to have found a man who had fallen into a shaft of Creekbraw's Mine, using some sort of remote viewing, and was able to recover stolen money by occult means. Was this conjuror Parson Wood? Maybe, but Polwhele seems to hint that it was a different person, with the following passage –

"In the last age, some of the rusticated clergy used to favour the popular superstition, by pretending to the power of laying ghosts... I could mention the names of several persons whose influence over their flock was solely attributable to this circumstance. By far other means, we now endeavour to secure the good opinion of those who are committed to our care"

So, who was this mysterious "celebrated Ladock conjuror"? I doubt we will ever know for sure, and it is probable that Parson William Wood himself was the source for these anonymous enigmatic tales.

The Legend of St Ciarán/Piran

Ciarán was born on Cape Clear Island, Co. Cork situated off Ireland's south coast, in the sixth century AD. Throughout his life he was widely renowned for his miraculous deeds and his love of the natural world. Nevertheless, groups of Irish kings were afraid of his powers and were jealous of his influence amongst the people. On a wild and stormy day, Ciarán was chained to a millstone, and thrown from the top of a high cliff into the sea below. The blustery wind was blowing a deadly gale, the sky was black with thunderclouds and the dark stormy sea was a maelstrom, white with foam, and swollen with massive waves.

As Ciarán was hurtling towards certain death the sun broke through the clouds, and instantly the winds abated and the raging stormy sea became calm. As the stone hit the sea it floated, hundreds in the crowd above, seeing Ciarán alive on the floating stone, were immediately converted to Christianity.

Wind and weather remained favourable for our reluctant spiritual hero, and after many days at sea, Ciarán landed safely on the beach that bears his name today -

Perranporth, meaning the cove or harbour of Piran. In the vast, remote and lofty sand dunes, overlooking the Celtic Sea, Ciarán built a cell and a small church. His first converts to Christianity were a fox, a badger and a bear. The Cornish people flocked to him as news of his teaching spread. It is alleged that he lived to the age of 206, at which time he still had all his teeth, perfect eyesight and showed no sign of old age. He is reputed to have died in a state of drunkenness by falling down a well. Legend states that he is buried at his Oratory in the dunes.

The etymology of Piran?

The letter C in Irish becomes P in the Cornish language. For example, the Irish word *cenn* meaning head becomes *penn* in Cornish, as in *Pentire*, Cornish language for headland. So, it is easy to see why Ciarán became known as Piran in Cornwall. St Piran's Oratory can still be viewed in the shifting sand dunes, and has recently been uncovered by archaeologists. It is hoped that the ancient building will be preserved and maybe future generations will be able to freely visit this incredibly important early medieval site of cultural, spiritual and historic importance. Nearby stands the 2.5 metre tall ancient three holed cross of St Piran.

This once flourishing Celtic Christian community of Piran would have rivalled Iona and Lindisfarne in its size and stature. These days St Piran is widely regarded as the patron saint of Cornwall and his feast on 5th March is a day of celebration across the Duchy and in Cornish Diaspora across the world. His flag is a white cross on a black background, said to depict the moment that Piran discovered tin, which poured from his blackened hearth-stone. Today the flag is proudly flown across the historic nation of Cornwall.

The Longstone - A Cornish Legend

In the parish of St. Mabyn, in East Cornwall, and on the high road from Bodmin to Camelford, is a group of houses (one of them yet a smith's shop) known by the name of Longstone. The curious traveller passing by inquires the *raison d'etre* of such a name, for there is no tall monolith, such as are not uncommon in Cornwall, to be seen near it. Let the reason be here fixed on the pages of *Notes & Queries.*

In lack of records, I may say "in the days of King Arthur there lived in Cornwall" a smith. This smith was a keen fellow, who made and mended the ploughs and harrows, shod the horses of his neighbours, and was generally serviceable. He had also great skill in farriery and in the general management and cure of sick cattle. He could also extract the stubbornest tooth, even if the jaw resisted and some gyrations around the anvil were required.

There seems ever to have been ill blood between devil and smith, *teste* Dunstan and others, and so it was between the fiend and the smith-farrier-dentist of St. Mabyn. At night, there were many and fierce disputes between them in the smithy. The smith, as the rustics tell, always got the advantage of his adversary, and gave him better than he brought. This success, however, only fretted old Nick and spurred him on to further encounter. What the exact matter of controversy on this particular occasion was is not remembered, but it was agreed to settle it by some wager, some trial of strength and skill. A two-acre field was near, and the smith challenged the devil to the reaping of each his acre in the shortest time. The match came off, and the devil was beaten; for the smith had beforehand stealthily stuck here and there over his opponent's acre some harrow tines or teeth.

The two started well, but soon the strong swing of the fiend's scythe was being brought up frequently by some obstruction, and as frequently required the whetstone. The dexterous and agile smith went on smoothly with his acre, and was soon unmistakably gaining. The devil, enraged at his certain discomfiture, hurled his whetstone at his rival, and flew off. The whetstone, thrown with great violence, after sundry whirls in the air, fell upright into the soil to a great depth, and there remained a witness against the evil one for ages. The devil avoided the neighbourhood while it stood. In an evil hour the farmer at Treblethick near set his heart upon the Longstone, for there were gate-posts and door-posts to be had out of it, and he threw it down. That night the enemy returned, and has haunted the neighbourhood ever since.

The destroyer of this fine monolith is a near neighbour of mine, who, showing no compunction, tells me that its overthrow was about thirty years ago. It was of granite, and consequently brought hither from a distance, for the local stone is a friable slate. It yielded four large gate-posts, gave spans to a small bridge, and left much granite remaining.

How Jan Brewer was Piskey-laden

The moon was near her setting as a tall, broad-shouldered man called Jan Brewer was walking home to Constantine Bay to his cottage on the edge of a cliff.

He was singing an old song to himself as he went along, and he sang till he drew near the ruins of Constantine Church, standing on a sandy common near the bay. As he grew near the remains of this ancient church, which were clearly seen in the moon-shine, he thought he heard someone laughing, but he was not quite sure, for the sea was roaring on the beach below the common, and the waves were making a loud noise as they dashed up the great headland of Trevose.

'I was mistaken; 'twas nobody laughing,' said Jan to himself, and he walked on again, singing as before; and he sang till he came near a gate, which opened into a field leading to his cottage, but when he got there he could not see the gate or the gateway.

'I was so taken up with singing the old song, that I must have missed my way,' he said again to himself. 'I'll go back to the head of the common and start afresh,' which he did and when he got to the place where his gate ought to have been, he could not find it to save his life.

' I must be clean mazed' he cried. 'I have never got out of my reckoning before, nor missed finding my way to our gate, even when the night has been as dark as pitch. It isn't at all dark to-night; I can see Trevose Head - looking across the bay, and yet I can't see my own little gate! But I en't a-going to be done; I'll go round and round this common till I do find my gate.'

And round and round the common he went, but find his gate he could not.

Every time he passed the ruins of the church a laugh came up from the pool below the ruins, and once he thought he saw a dancing light on the edge of the pool, where a lot of reeds and rushes were growing.

'The Little Man in the Lantern is about to-night' he said to himself, as he glanced at the pool. 'But I never knew he was given to laughing before.'

Once more he went round the common, and when he had passed the ruins he heard giggling and laughing, this time quite close to him; and looking down on the grass, he saw to his astonishment hundreds of Little Men and Little Women with tiny lights in their hands, which they were flinking about as they laughed and giggled.

The Little Men wore stocking-caps, the colour of ripe briar berries, and grass-green coats, and the Little Women had on old grandmother cloaks of the same vivid hue as the Wee Men's coats, and they also wore fascinating little scarlet hoods.

'I believe the great big chap sees us,' said one of the Little Men, catching sight of Jan's astonished face. 'He must be Piskey-eyed, and we did not know it.'

' Is he really?' cried one of the Dinky Women. 'Tis a pity,' as the Little Man nodded. 'But we'll have our game over him all the same.'

'That we will,' cried all the Little Men and Little Women in one voice: and, forming a ring round the great tall fellow, they began to dance round him, laughing, giggling and flashing up their lights as they danced.

They went round him so fast that poor Jan was quite bewildered, and whichever way he looked there were these Little Men and Little Women giggling up into his bearded face. And when he tried to break through their ring they went before him and behind him, making a game over him, he said!

He was at their mercy and they knew it; and when they saw the great fellow's misery, they only laughed and giggled the more.

'We've got him!' they cried to each other, and they said it with such gusto and with such a comical expression on their tiny brown faces, that Jan, bewildered as he was, and tired with going round the common so many times, could not help laughing, they looked so very funny, particularly when the Little Women winked up at him from under their little scarlet hoods.

The Piskeys for they were Piskeys, hurried him down the common, dancing round him all the time; and when he got there he felt so mizzy-mazey with those tiny whirling figures going round and round him like a whirligig, that he did not know whether he was standing on his head or his heels.

He was also in a bath of perspiration 'sweating leaking', he expressed it and, putting his hand in his pocket to take out a handkerchief to mop his face, he remembered having been told that, if ever he got Piskey-laden, he must turn his coat pockets inside out, when he would be free at once from his Piskey tormentors. He immediately acted on this suggestion, and in a minute or less his coat-pockets were hanging out, and all the Little Men and the Little Women had vanished, and there, right in front of him, he saw his own gate! He lost no time in opening it, and in a very short time was in his thatched cottage on the cliff.

Encounter at Dolcoath Mine

We entered the blacksmith's shed by the door I have mentioned, which fronted the high road, and had just finished changing our dress, when we heard a tremendous racket outside. We ran to the door, and there was a little horseman on a night-black nag, galloping furiously in front of the smithy.

In a moment the horse was checked, and back came the rash rider again, sweeping by like the wind. But instead of continuing on the carriage road, the smoking steed dashed over the heaps of rubbish behind the shed, where a horse had never been known to have gone before. Round, and round, and round the shed it rushed at a frantic pace, each time faster than before. as if the weird animal had wings. I could see no whip in the rider's hand, or bridle-rein, no saddle-stirrup or spur, neither could I discover any face to the horseman. The mystic horse then dashed by us so near that the wind it stirred rushed in our faces. On it went in the very direction of our home, over the road we walked.

The smithy stood in a mineral valley known as Bottom Hill, and its sides were very steep, so that it was no easy task to go up them. The carriage road wound along its side, running on a considerable length until it reached the top. There was, however, a footpath for passengers almost in a direct line from the lowest part of the valley to the very edge of the hill. At the distance of every few yards there were flights of steps, so as to surmount it more easily. But a horse to go up that way would be almost like scaling a cliff. What was our surprise, then, when this hazardous horseman, but a few feet in advance of us, dashed right up over these steps! As he leaped from level to level, and from stone to stone, the black horse seemed standing upright on its hind legs. No sound was heard, no ' crack of whip, no breathing of the jaded beast, but all was still as death.

Of course, the wild horse and its wilder rider reached the high-road on the top of the valley long before we did, though we paced on considerably faster than we were wont. I felt no fear, and hardly expected to see it again, but had resolved that, should it make its appearance, to call out boldly and ask what it wanted. Exactly as we reached the last step of the footpath, which would land us on the main road, there was the black horse and its sooty rider coming full tilt in our faces! I had an opportunity, for a second, to examine the horseman; for by this time the moon had risen, and the light was tolerably good. He seemed as black as ink, armless and legless, and no bigger than a farmer's watchdog. He was bent forward upon the horse's neck, so that he was almost double. I could see no face or features of any kind - no whip, or bridle, or saddle-girth. But down he came sweeping like a storm-wave. We stepped quickly aside, and I shouted, "Good night!" but there was no reply, no recognition of our presence, or murmur of any kind. On went the black horse galloping into the midnight, on, on! For several minutes, we heard the animal's hoofs rattling and ringing upon the road towards Tuckingmill; and then all was silent, and we saw it no more. What it was I have never discovered to this day, but it was no ghost.

The Mermaid's Vengeance

In one of the deep valleys of the parish of Perranzabuloe, which are remarkable for their fertility, and especially for the abundance of fruit which the orchards produce, lived in days long ago, amidst a rudely-civilised people, a farmer's labourer, his wife, with one child, a daughter. The man and woman were equally industrious. The neatly white-washed walls of their mud-built cottage, the well-kept gravelled paths, and carefully-weeded beds of their small garden, in which flowers were cultivated for ornament, and vegetables for use, proclaimed at once the character of the inmates. In contrast with the neighbouring cottages, this one, although smaller than many others, had a superior aspect, and the occupiers of it exhibited a strong contrast to those peasants and miners amidst whom they dwelt.

Pennaluna, as the man was called, or Penna the Proud, as he was, in no very friendly spirit, named by his less thoughtful and more impulsive fellows, was, as we have said, a farmer's labourer. His master was a wealthy yeoman, and he, after many years' experience, was so convinced of the exceeding industry and sterling honesty of Penna, that he made him the manager of an outlying farm in this parish, under the hind (or hine - the Saxon pronunciation is still retained in the West of England), or general supervisor of this and numerous other extensive farms.

Penna was too great a favourite with the Squire to be a favourite of the hind's; he was evidently jealous of him, and from not being himself a man of very strict principles, he hated the unobtrusive goodness of his underling, and was constantly on the watch to discover some cause of complaint. It was not, however, often that he was successful in this. Every task committed to the care of Penna, and he was often purposely overtasked, was executed with great care and dispatch. With the wife of Penna, however, the case was unfortunately different. Honour Penna was as industrious as her husband, and to him she was in all respects a helpmate. She had, however, naturally a proud spirit, and this had been encouraged in her youth by her parents. Honour was very pretty as a girl, and, indeed, she retained much beauty as a woman. The only education she received was the wild one of experience, and this within a very narrow circle. She grew an ignorant girl, amongst ignorant men and women, few of them being able to write their names, and scarcely any of them to read. There was much native grace about her, and she was flattered by the young men, and envied by the young women, of the village, the envy and the flattery being equally pleasant to her. In the same village was born, and brought up, Tom Chenalls, who had, in the course of years, become hind to the Squire. Tom, as a young man, had often expressed himself fond of Honour, but he was always distasteful to the village maiden, and eventually, while yet young, she was married to Pennaluna, who came from the southern coast, bringing with him the recommendation of being a stranger, and an exceedingly hard-working man, who was certain to earn bread, and something more, for his wife and family. In the relations in which these people were now placed towards each other, Chenalls had the opportunity of acting ungenerously towards the Pennas. The man bore this uncomplainingly, but the woman frequently quarrelled with him whom she felt was an enemy, and whom she still regarded but as her equal. Chenalls was a skilled farmer, and hence was of considerable value to the Squire; but although he was endured for his farming knowledge and his business habits, he was never a favourite with his employer. Penna, on the contrary, was an especial favourite, and the evidences of this were so often brought strikingly under the observation of Chenalls, that it increased the irritation of his hate, for it amounted to that. For years things went on thus. There was the tranquil suffering of an oppressed spirit manifested in Penna, the angry words and actions of his wife towards the oppressor, and, at the same time, as she with much fondness studied to make their humble home comfortable for her husband, she reviled him not unfrequently for the meek spirit with which he endured his petty, but still trying, wrongs. The hind dared not venture on any positive act of wrong towards those people, yet he lost no chance of annoying them, knowing that the Squire's partiality for Penna would not allow him to venture beyond certain bounds, even in this direction.

Penna's solace was his daughter. She had now reached her eighteenth year, and with the well-developed form of a woman, she united the simplicity of a child. Selina, as she was named, was in many respects beautiful. Her features were regular, and had they been lighted up with more mental fire, they would have been beautiful; but the constant repose, the want of animation, left her face merely a pretty one. Her skin was beautifully white, and transparent to the blue veins which traced their ways beneath it, to the verge of that delicacy which indicates disease; but it did not pass that verge. Selina was full of health, as her well moulded form at once showed, and her clear blue eye distinctly told. At times there was a lovely tint upon the cheek, not the hectic of consumptive beauty, but a pure rosy dye, suffused by the healthy life stream, when it flowed the fastest.

The village gossips, who were always busy with their neighbours, said strange things of this girl. Indeed, it was commonly reported that the real child of the Pennas was a remarkably plain child, in every respect a different being from Selina. The striking difference between the infant and the woman was variously explained by the knowing ones. Two stories were, however, current for miles around the country. One was, that Selina's mother was constantly seen gathering dew in the morning, with which to wash her child, and that the fairies on the Towens had, in pure malice, aided her in giving a temporary beauty to the girl, that it might lead to her betrayal into crime. Why this malice, was never clearly made out. The other story was, that Honour Penna constantly bathed the child in a certain pool, amidst the arched rocks of Perran, which was a favourite resort of the mermaids; that on one occasion the child, as if in a paroxysm of joy, leapt from her arms into the water, and disappeared. The mother, as may well be supposed, suffered a momentary agony of terror; but presently the babe swam up to the surface of the water, its little face more bright and beautiful than it had ever been before. Great was the mother's joy, and also, as the gossips say, great her surprise at the sudden change in the appearance of her offspring. The mother knew no difference in the child whom she pressed lovingly to her bosom, but all the aged crones in the parish declared it to be a changeling. This tale lived its day; but, as the girl grew on to womanhood, and showed none of the special qualifications belonging either to fairies or mermaids, it was almost forgotten. The uncomplaining father had solace for all his sufferings in wandering over the beautiful sands with his daughter. Whether it was when the summer seas fell in musical undulations on the shore, or when, stirred by the winter tempests, the great Atlantic waves came up in grandeur, and lashed the resisting sands in giant rage, those two enjoyed the solitude. Hour after hour, from the setting sun time, until the clear cold moon flooded the ocean with her smiles of light, would the father and child walk these sands. They seemed never to weary of them and the ocean.

Almost every morning, throughout the milder seasons, Selina was in the habit of bathing, and wild tales were told of the frantic joy with which she would play with the breaking billows. Sometimes floating over, and almost dancing on the crests of the waves, at other times rushing under them, and allowing the breaking waters to beat her to the sands, as though they were loving arms, endeavouring to encircle her form. Certain it is, that Selina greatly enjoyed her bath, but all the rest must be regarded as the creations of the imagination. The most eager to give a construction unfavourable to the simple mortality of the maiden was, however, compelled to acknowledge that there was no evidence in her general conduct to support their surmises. Selina, as an only child, fared the fate of others who are unfortunately so placed, and was, as the phrase is, spoiled. She certainly was allowed to follow her own inclinations without any check. Still her inclinations were bounded to working in the garden, and to leading her father to the sea-shore. Honour Penna, sometimes, it is true, did complain that Selina could not be trusted with the most ordinary domestic duty. Beyond this, there was one other cause of grief, that was, the increasing dislike which Selina exhibited towards entering a church. The girl, notwithstanding the constant excuses of being sick, suffering from headache, having a pain in her side, and the like, was often taken, notwithstanding, by her mother to the church. It is said that she always shuddered as she passed the church-stile, and again on stepping from the porch into the church itself. When once within the house of prayer she evinced no peculiar liking or disliking, observing respectfully all the rules during the performance of the church-service, and generally sleeping, or seeming to sleep, during the sermon. Selina Pennaluna had reached her eighteenth year; she was admired by many of the young men of the parish, but, as if surrounded by a spell, she appeared to keep them all at a distance from her. About this time, a nephew to the Squire, a young soldier, who had been wounded in the wars, came into Cornwall to heal his wounds, and recover health, which had suffered in a trying campaign.

This young man, Walter Trewoofe, was a rare specimen of manhood. Even now, shattered as he was by the combined influences of wounds, an unhealthy climate, and dissipation, he could not but be admired for fineness of form, dignity of carriage, and masculine beauty. It was, however, but too evident, that this young man was his own idol, and that he expected everyone to bow down with him, and worship it. His uncle was proud of Walter, and although the old gentleman could not fail to see many faults, yet he regarded them as the follies of youth, and trusted to their correction with the increase of years and experience. Walter, who was really suffering severely, was ordered by his surgeon, at first, to take short walks on the sea-shore, and, as he gained strength, to bathe. He was usually driven in his uncle's pony-carriage to the edge of the sands. Then dismounting he would walk for a short time, and quickly wearing, return in his carriage to the luxuriant couches at the manor-house.

On some of those occasions Walter had observed the father and daughter taking their solitary ramble. He was struck with the quiet beauty of the girl, and seized an early opportunity of stopping Penna to make some general inquiry respecting the bold and beautiful coast. From time to time they thus met, and it would have been evident to any observer that Walter did not so soon weary of the sands as formerly, and that Selina was not displeased with the flattering things he said to her. Although the young soldier had hitherto led a wild life, it would appear as if for a considerable period the presence of goodness had repressed every tendency to evil in his ill-regulated heart. He continued, therefore, for some time playing with his own feelings and those of the childlike being who presented so much of romance, combined with the most homely tameness, of character. Selina, it is true, had never yet seen Walter except in the presence of her father, and it is questionable if she had ever for one moment had a warmer feeling than that of the mere pleasure - a silent pride - that a gentleman, at once so handsome, so refined, and the nephew of her father's master, should pay her any attention. Evil eyes were watching with wicked earnestness the growth of passion, and designing hearts were beating quicker with a consciousness that they should eventually rejoice in the downfall of innocence. Tom Chenalls hoped that he might achieve a triumph, if he could but once asperse the character of Selina. He took his measures accordingly. Having noticed the change in the general conduct of his master's nephew, he argued that this was due to the refining influence of a pure mind, acting on one more than ordinarily impressionable to either evil or good.

Walter rapidly recovered health, and with renewed strength the manly energy of his character began to develop itself. He delighted in horse-exercise, and Chenalls had always the best horse on the farms at his disposal. He was a good shot, and Chenalls was his guide to the best shooting-grounds. He sometimes fished, and Chenalls knew exactly where the choicest trout and the richest salmon were to be found. In fact, Chenalls entered so fully into the tastes of the young man, that

Walter found him absolutely necessary to him to secure the enjoyments of a country life.

Having established this close intimacy, Chenalls never lost an opportunity of talking with Walter respecting Selina Penna. He soon satisfied himself that Walter, like most other young men who had led a dissipated life, had but a very low estimate of women generally. Acting upon this, he at first insinuated that Selina's innocence was but a mask, and at length he boldly assured Walter that the cottage girl was to be won by him with a few words, and that then he might put her aside at any time as a prize to some low-born peasant. Chenalls never failed to impress on Walter the necessity of keeping his uncle in the most perfect darkness, and of blinding the eyes of Selina's parents. Penna was, so thought Chenalls, easily managed, but there was more to be feared from the wife. Walter, however, with much artifice, having introduced himself to Honour Penna, employed the magic of that flattery, which, being properly applied, seldom fails to work its way to the heart of a weak-minded woman. He became an especial favourite with Honour, and the blinded mother was ever pleased at the attention bestowed with so little assumption, as she thought, of pride, on her daughter, by one so much above them. Walter eventually succeeded in separating occasionally, though not often, Penna and his daughter. The witching whispers of unholy love were poured into the trusting ear. Guileless herself, this child-woman suspected no guile in others, least of all in one whom she had been taught to look upon as a superior being to herself. Amongst the villagers, the constant attention of Walter Trewoofe was the subject of gossip, and many an old proverb was quoted by the elder women, ill-naturedly, and implying that evil must come of this intimacy, Tom Chenalls was now employed by Walter to contrive some means by which he could remove Penna for a period from home. He was not long in doing this. He lent every power of his wicked nature to aid the evil designs of the young soldier, and thus he brought about that separation of father and child which ended in her ruin.

Near the Land's End the squire possessed some farms, and one of them was reported to be in such a state of extreme neglect, through the drunkenness and consequent idleness of the tenant, that Chenalls soon obtained permission to take the farm from this occupier, which he did in the most unscrupulous disregard for law or right. It was then suggested that the only plan by which a desirable occupier could be found, would be to get the farm and farm-buildings into good condition, and that Penna, of all men, would be the man to bring this quickly about. The squire was pleased with the plan. Penna was sent for by him, and was proud of the confidence which his master reposed in him. There was some sorrow on his leaving home. He subsequently said that he had had many warnings not to go, but he felt that he dared not disoblige a master who had trusted him so far, so he went.

Walter needed not any urging on the part of Chenalls, though he was always ready to apply the spur when there was the least evidence of the sense of right asserting itself in the young man's bosom. Week after week passed on. Walter had rendered himself a necessity to Selina. Without her admirer, the world was cold and colourless. With him all was sunshine and glowing tints.

Three months passed thus away, and during that period it had only been possible for Penna to visit his home twice. The father felt that something like a spirit of evil stood between him and his daughter. There was no outward evidence of any change, but there was an inward sense - undefined, yet deeply felt like an overpowering fear, that some wrong had been done. On parting, Penna silently but earnestly prayed that the deep dread might be removed from his mind. There was an aged fisherman, who resided in a small cottage built on the sands, who possessed all the superstitions of his class. This old man had formed a father's liking for the simple-hearted maiden, and he had persuaded himself that there really was some foundation for the tales which the gossips told. To the fisherman, Walter Trewoofe was an evil genius. He declared that no good ever came to him, if he met Walter when he was about to go to sea. With this feeling, he curiously watched the young man and maiden, and he, in after days, stated his conviction that he had seen merry maidens rising from the depth of the waters, and floating under the billows to watch Selina and her lover. He has also been heard to say that on more than one occasion Walter himself had been terrified by sights and sounds. Certain, however, it is, these were insufficient and the might of evil passions were more powerful than any of the protecting influences of the unseen world.

Another three months had gone by, and Walter Trewoofe had disappeared from Perranzabuloe. He had launched into the gay world of the metropolis, and rarely, if ever, dreamed of the deep sorrow which was weighing down the heart he had betrayed Penna returned home, his task was done, and Chenalls had no reason for keeping him any longer from his wife and daughter. Clouds gathered slowly but unremittingly around him. His daughter retired into herself no longer as of old reposing her whole soul on her father's heart. His wife was somewhat changed too, she had some secret in her heart which she feared to tell. The home he had left was not the home to which he had returned. It soon became evident that some shock had shaken the delicate frame of his daughter. She pined rapidly; and Penna was awakened to a knowledge of the cause by the rude rejoicing of Chenalls, who declared "that all people who kept themselves so much above other people were sure to be pulled down." On one occasion, he so far tempted Penna with sneers, at his having hope to secure the young squire for a son-in-law, that the long-enduring man broke forth and administered a severe blow upon his tormentor. This was duly reported to the squire, and added thereto was a magnified story of a trap which had been set by the Penna to catch young Walter; it was represented that even now they intended to press their claims, on account of grievous wrongs upon them, whereas it could be proved that Walter was guiltless - that he was indeed the innocent victim of designing people, who though to make money out of their assumed misfortune. The squire made his inquiries, and there were not a few who eagerly seized the opportunity to gain the friendship of Chenalls by representing this family to have been hypocrites of the deepest dye; and the poor girl especially was now loaded with a weight of iniquities of which she had no knowledge. All this ended in the dismissal of Penna from the Squire's service, and in his being deprived of the cottage in which he had taken so much pride. Although thrown out upon the world a disgraced man, Penna faced his difficulties manfully. He cast off, as it were, the primitive simplicity of his character, and evidently worked with a firm resolve to beat down his sorrows. He was too good a workman to remain long unemployed; and although his new home was not his happy home as of old, there was no repining heard from his lips. Weaker and weaker grew Selina, and it soon became evident to all, that if she came from a spirit-world, to a spirit-world she must soon return. Grief filled the hearts of her parents, it prostrated her mother, but the effects of severe labour, and the efforts of a settled mind, appeared to tranquilise the breast of her father. Time passed on, the wounds of the soul grew deeper, and there lay, on a low bed, from which she had not strength to move, the fragile form of youth with the countenance of age. The body was almost powerless, but there beamed from the eye the evidences of a spirit getting free from the chains of clay.

The dying girl was sensible of the presence of creations other than mortal, and with these she appeared to hold converse, and to derive solace from the communion. Penna and his wife alternately watched through the night hours by the side of their loved child, and anxiously did they mark the moment when the tide turned, in the full belief that she would be taken from them when the waters of the ocean began to recede from the shore. Thus, days passed on, and eventually the sunlight of a summer morning shone in through the small window of this humble cottage, on a dead mother and a living babe.

The dead was buried in the churchyard on the sands, and the living went on their ways, some rejoicingly and some in sorrow.

Once more Walter Trewoofe appeared in Perran-on-the-sands. Penna would have sacrificed him to his hatred; he emphatically protested that he had lived only to do so; but the good priest of the Oratory contrived to lay the devil who had possession, and to convince Penna that the Lord would, in His own good time, and in His own way, avenge the bitter wrong. Tom Chenalls had his hour of triumph; but from the day on which Selina died everything went wrong. The crops failed, the cattle died, hay-stacks and corn-ricks caught fire, cows slipped their calves, horses fell lame, or stumbled and broke their knees, a succession of evils steadily pursued him. Trials find but a short resting-place with the good; they may be bowed to the earth with the weight of a sudden sorrow, but they look to heaven, and their elasticity is restored. The evil-minded are crushed at once, and grovel on the ground in irremediable misery. That Chenalls fled to drink in his troubles appeared but the natural result to a man of his character. This unfitted him for his duties, and he was eventually dismissed from his situation. Notwithstanding that the Squire refused to listen to the appeals in favour of Chenalls, which were urged upon him by Walter, and that indeed he forbade his nephew to countenance "the scoundrel" in any way, Walter still continued his friend. By his means Tom Chenalls secured a small cottage on the cliff, and around it a little cultivated ground, the produce of which was his only visible means of support. That lonely cottage was the scene, however, of drunken carousals, and there the vicious young men, and the no less vicious young women, of the district, went after nightfall, and kept "high carnival" of sin. Walter Trewoofe came frequently amongst them; and as his purse usually defrayed the costs of a debauch, he was regarded by all with especial favour.

One midnight, Walter, who had been dancing and drinking for some hours, left the cottage wearied with his excesses, and although not drunk, he was much excited with wine. His pathway lay along the edge of the cliffs, amidst bushes of furze and heath, and through several irregular, zigzag ways. There were lateral paths striking off from one side of the main path, and leading down to the sea-shore. Although it was moonlight, without being actually aware of the error, Walter wandered into one of those; and before he was awake to his mistake, he found himself on the sands. He cursed his stupidity, and, uttering a blasphemous oath, he turned to retrace his steps.

The most exquisite music which ever flowed from human ups fell on his ear; he paused to listen, and collecting his unbalanced thoughts, he discovered that it was the voice of a woman singing a melancholy dirge

"The stars are beautiful, when bright

They are mirror'd in the sea;

But they are pale beside that light

Which was so beautiful to me.

My angel child, my earth-born girl,

From all your kindred riven,

By the base deeds of a selfish churl,

And to a sand-grave driven!

How shall I win thee back to ocean?

How canst thou quit thy grave,

To share again the sweet emotion

Of gliding through the wave?"

Walter, led by the melancholy song, advanced slowly along the sands. He discovered that the sweet, soft sounds proceeded from the other side of a mass of rocks, which project far out over the sands, and that now, at low-water, there was no difficulty in walking around it. Without hesitation he did so, and he beheld, sitting at the mouth of a cavern, one of the most beautiful women he had ever beheld. She continued her song, looking upwards to the stars, not appearing to notice the intrusion of a stranger. Walter stopped, and gazed on the lovely image before him with admiration and wonder, mingled with something of terror. He dared not speak, but fixed, as if by magic, he stood gazing on. After a few minutes, the maiden, suddenly perceiving that a man was near her, uttered a piercing shriek, and made as if to fly into the cavern. Walter sprang forward and seized her by the arm, exclaiming, "Not yet, my pretty maiden, not yet." She stood still in the position of flight, with her arm behind her, grasped by Walter, and turning round her head, her dark eyes beamed with unnatural lustre upon him. Impressionable he had ever been, but never had he experienced anything so entrancing, and at the same time so painful, as that gaze. It was Selina's face looking lovingly upon him, but it seemed to possess some new power - a might of mind from which he felt it was impossible for him to escape. Walter slackened his hold, and slowly allowed the arm to fall from his hand. The maiden turned fully round upon him. "Go!" she said. He could not move.

"Go, man!" she repeated. He was powerless.

"Go to the grave where the sinless one sleepeth!

Bring her cold corpse where her guarding one weepeth;

Look on her, love her again, ay betray her,

And wreath with false smiles the pale face of her slayer!

Go, go now, and feel the full force of my sorrow!

For the glut of my vengeance there cometh a morrow."

Walter was statue-like, and he awoke from this trance-like state only when the waves washed his feet, and he became aware that even now it was only by wading through the waters that he could return around the point of rocks. He was alone. He called; no one answered. He sought wildly, as far as he now dared, amidst the rocks, but the lovely woman was nowhere to be discovered.

There was no real danger on such a night as this; therefore, Walter walked fearlessly through the gentle waves, and recovered the pathway up from the sands. More than once he thought he heard a rejoicing laugh, which was echoed in the rocks, but no one was to be seen. Walter reached his home and bed, but he found no sleep; and in the morning, he arose with a sense of wretchedness which was entirely new to him. He feared to make any one of his rough companions a confidant, although he felt this would have relieved his heart. He therefore nursed the wound which he now felt, until a bitter remorse clouded his existence. After some days, he was impelled to visit the grave of the lost one, and in the fullness of the most selfish sorrow, he sat on the sands and shed tears. The priest of the Oratory observed him, and knowing Walter Trewoofe, hesitated not to inquire into his cause of sorrow. His heart was opened to the holy man, and the strange tale was told

- the only result being, that the priest felt satisfied it was but a vivid dream, which had resulted from a brain over-excited by drink. He, however, counselled the young man, giving him some religious instruction, and dismissed him with his blessing. There was relief in this. For some days Walter did not venture to visit his old haunt, the cottage of Chenalls. Since he could not be lost to his companions without greatly curtailing their vicious enjoyments, he was hunted up by Chenalls, and again enticed within the circle. His absence was explained on the plea of illness. Walter was, however, an altered man; there was not the same boisterous hilarity as formerly. He no longer abandoned himself without restraint to the enjoyments of the time. If he ever, led on by his thoughtless and rough-natured friends, assumed for a moment his usual mirth, it was checked by some invisible power. On such occasions, he would turn deadly pale, look anxiously around, and fail back, as if ready to faint, on the nearest seat. Under these influences, he lost health. His uncle, who was really attached to his nephew, although he regretted his dissolute conduct, became now seriously alarmed. Physicians were consulted in vain; the young man pined, and the old gossips came to the conclusion that Walter Trewoofe was ill-wished, and there was a general feeling that Penna or his wife was at the bottom of it. Walter, living really on one idea, and that one the beautiful face which was, and yet was not, that of Selina, resolved again to explore the spot on which he had met this strange being, of whom nothing could be learned by any of the covert inquiries he made. He lingered long ere he could resolve on the task; but wearied, worn by the oppression of one undefined idea, in which an intensity of love was mixed with a shuddering fear, he at last gathered sufficient courage to seize an opportunity for again going to the cavern. On this occasion, there being no moon, the night was dark, but the stars shone brightly from a sky, cloudless, save a dark mist which hung heavily over the western horizon. Every spot of ground being familiar to him, who, boy and man, had traced it over many times, the partial darkness presented no difficulty. Walter had scarcely reached the level sands, which were left hard by the retiring tide, then he heard again the same magical voice as before. But now the song was a joyous one, the burthen of it being

"Join all hands

Might and main,

Weave the sands,

Form a chain,

He, my lover,

Comes again!"

He could not entirely dissuade himself but that he heard this repeated by many voices; but he put the thought aside, referring it, as well he might, to the numerous echoes from the cavernous openings in the cliffs.

He reached the eastern side of the dark mass of rocks, from the point of which the tide was slowly subsiding. The song had ceased, and a low moaning sound - the soughing of the wind passed along the shore. Walter trembled with fear, and was on the point of returning, when a most flute-like murmur rose from the other side of the rocky barrier, which was presently moulded into words

"From your couch of glistering pearl,

Slowly, softly, come away;

Our sweet earth-child, lovely girl,

Died this day, died this day."

Memory told Walter that truly was it the anniversary of Selina Pennaluna's death, and to him every gentle wave falling on the shore sang, or murmured

"Died this day, died this day."

The sand was left dry around the point of the rocks, and Walter impelled by a power which he could not control, walked onward. The moment he appeared on the western side of the rock, a wild laugh burst into the air, as if from the deep cavern before him, at the entrance of which sat the same beautiful being whom he had formerly met. There was now an expression of rare joy on her face, her eyes glistened with delight, and she extended her arms. as if to welcome him.

"Was it ever your wont to move so slowly towards your loved one?"

Walter heard it was Selina's voice. He saw it was Selina's features; but he was conscious it was not Selina's form.

"Come, sit beside me, Walter, and let us talk of love."

He sat down without a word, and looked into the maiden's face with a vacant expression of fondness. Presently she placed her hand upon his heart; a shudder passed through his frame; but having passed, he felt no more pain, but a rare intensity of delight. The maiden wreathed her arm around his neck, drew Walter towards her, and then he remembered how often he had acted thus towards Selina. She bent over him and looked into his eyes. In his mind's mirror, he saw himself looking thus into the eyes of his betrayed one.

"You loved her once?" said the maiden.

"I did indeed," answered Walter, with a sigh.

"As you loved her, so I love you," said the maiden, with a smile which shot like a poisoned dart through Walter's heart. She lifted the young man's head lovingly between her hands, and bending over him, pressed her lips upon and kissed his forehead, Walter curiously felt that although he was the kissed, yet that he was the kisser.

"Kisses," she said, "are as true at sea as they are false on land. You men kiss the earth-born maidens to betray them. The kiss of a sea-child is the seal of constancy. You are mine till death."

"Death!" almost shrieked Walter.

A full consciousness of his situation now broke upon Walter. He had heard the tales of the gossips respecting the mermaid origin of Selina; but he had laughed at them as an idle fancy. He now felt they were true. For hours Walter was compelled to sit by the side of his beautiful tormentor, every word of assumed love and rapture being a torture of the most exquisite kind to him. He could not escape from the arms which were wound around him. He saw the tide rising rapidly. He heard the deep voice of the winds coming over the sea from the far west. He saw that which appeared at first as a dark mist, shape itself into a dense black mass of cloud, and rise rapidly over the star-bedecked space above him. He saw by the brilliant edge of light which occasionally fringed the clouds that they were deeply charged with thunder. There was something sublime in the steady motion of the storm; and now the roll of the waves, which had been disturbed in the Atlantic, reached our shores, and the breakers fell thunderingly within a few feet of Walter and his companion. Paroxysms of terror shook him, and with each convulsion he felt himself grasped with still more ardour, and pressed so closely to the maiden's bosom, that he heard her heart dancing of joy.

At length, his terrors gave birth to words, and he implored her to let him go.

"The kiss of the sea-child is the seal of constancy." Walter vehemently implored forgiveness. He confessed his deep iniquity. He promised a life of penitence.

"Give me back the dead," said the maiden bitterly, and she planted another kiss, which seemed to pierce his brain by its coldness, upon his forehead.

The waves rolled around the rock on which they sat; they washed their seat. Walter was still in the female's grasp, and she lifted him to a higher ledge. The storm approached. Lightnings struck down from the heavens into the sands; and thunders roared along the iron cliffs. The mighty waves grew yet more rash, and washed up to this strange pair, who now sat on the highest pinnacle of the pile of rocks. Walter's terrors nearly overcame him; but he was roused by a liquid stream of fire, which positively hissed by him, followed immediately by a crash of thunder, which shook the solid earth. Tom Chenall's cottage on the cliff burst into a blaze, and Walter saw, from his place amidst the raging waters, a crowd of male and female roisterers rush terrified out upon the heath, to be driven back by the pelting storm. The climax of horrors appeared to surround Walter. He longed to end it in death, but he could not die. His senses were quickened. He saw his wicked companion and evil adviser struck to the ground, a blasted heap of ashes, by a lightning stroke, and at the same moment he and his companion were borne off the rock on the top of a mountainous wave, on which he floated; the woman holding him by the hair of his head, and singing in a rejoicing voice, which was like a silver bell heard amidst the deep base bellowing's of the storm -

"Come away, come away,
O'er the waters wild!
Our earth-born child
Died this day, died this day.
Come away, come away!
The tempest loud
Weaves the shroud
For him who did betray.
Come away, come away!
Beneath the wave
Lieth the grave
Of him we slay, him we slay.
Come away, come away!
He shall not rest
In earth's own breast
For many a day, many a day.
Come away, come away!
By billows to
From coast to coast,
Like deserted boat
His corpse shall float
Around the bay, around the bay."

Myriads of voices on that wretched night were heard amidst the roar of the storm. The waves were seen covered with a multitudinous host, who were tossing from one to the other the dying Walter Trewoofe, whose false heart thus endured the vengeance of the mermaid, who had, in the fondness of her soul, made the innocent child of humble parents the child of her adoption.

Several versions of this story have been given me. The general idea of the tale belongs to the north coast; but the fact of mermaidens taking innocents under their charge was common around the Lizard, and in some of the coves near the Land's End. *Robert Hunt.*

Available from www.spiritofalbionbooks.co.uk

Lundy Hole and the Devil

Nicholas Roscarrock recorded the following folklore from the remote Cornish peninsula between Wadebridge and Port Isaac. It concerns St Menefrida, patron of St Minver church and was first recorded during the early 17th century.

One fine day, whilst Menefrida was combing her hair by her ancient chapel and holy well at Tredrizzick, she was rudely confronted by the Devil, who appeared from the deep shadows of the local woods. She was so distressed by his astonishing apparition, that she threw her comb at him, striking the fiend with such force that he flew through the air and plunged into the ground at Topalundy, on the nearby coast. His violent landing created the great rupture, now known as Lundy Hole, sited high on the clifftop above Lundy Cove, Polzeath.

It is interesting to note that Roscarrock lived nearby at St Endellion, so one must assume this was an established folktale in his day.

Notes and References

Saints, Demons and Conjurors, retold by Alex Langstone. Article first published by Meyn Mamvro No. 93, Summer 2017. Folklore originally collected by William Bottrell and published as Legends of Ladock in Stories and Folklore of West Cornwall. 1880.

The Legend of St Ciarán/Piran, retold by Alex Langstone from the tale *How St Piran Came to Cornwall* in Legend Land, Vol. 1. Published by The Great Western Railway. 1922.

The Longstone: A Cornish Legend. Published by Thomas Quiller Couch, in Notes and Queries, April 23rd, 1883.

How Jan Brewer was Piskey-laden. Collected and published by Enys Tregarthen in North Cornwall Fairies and Legends. 1906.

Encounter at Dolcoath Mine. Extract from My Autobiography by John Harris. 1882.

The Mermaid's Vengeance. Collected and published by Robert Hunt in his Popular Romances of the West of England. 1865.

Lundy Hole and the Devil, retold by Alex Langstone, originally collected circa 1600 and published in Lives of the Saints: Cornwall and Devon by Nicholas Roscarrock.

#0110 - 260717 - C0 - 210/148/2 - PB - DID1903484